ABUSE AND NEGLECT OF

Our present day understanding and foc
neglect of senior citizens has been an e
understanding that has grown since the
it, in the 1960's, was a growing knowledge of the issues that were responsible for family violence, and the abuse of women and children specifically (see, for example, Quinn and Tomita 1997 did research; Hudson 1986; and Steinmetz 1977/1978).

As advocacy groups, academic research groups, therapists, the psychological association, political law makers and churches began to help bring attention to this social ill; our society started to evolve in a positive direction and get deeper into the issue of abuse. We have changed in our understanding of "abuse" to realize there is more than just physical abuse. We understand that "emotional abuse," "verbal abuse," "psychological abuse," "financial abuse," "name calling," and "shaming abuse," can all have devastating and long-term effects on the sensitive nature of human beings. These are all things that are "done to" a person. Furthermore, "neglect" (not "doing" anything, but just the opposite - doing nothing. Not taking or doing an action.) has been brought into the picture of unhealthy behavior because it is something that can also be as harmful or dangerous as physically beating on someone. Or, as Christianity puts it: we commit sins of commission and omission. We can make mistakes by doing things, and we can make mistakes by not doing things we should be doing.

Once professionals had looked at the family dynamics of abuse and neglect, society began to look at abuse and neglect within the context of institutions such as nursing homes, long term care facilities and retirement homes. It is easy for forms of abuse and neglect to creep into both families and institutions. We must always keep a vigilant eye and ear attuned to signs of abuse in our communities – for it is always there, lurking like a burglar in the dark shadows - ready to steal away the 'quality of

ABUSE AND NEGLECT OF OLDER ADULTS

life' and 'peace of mind' of citizens both young and old. When we see it, we must do something, regardless of the consequences to our comfort. Sometimes our temptation is to be silent in the face of injustice or abuse and not 'get involved' or not 'rock the boat.' We must resist the temptation to 'look the other way' when it comes to injustice or abuse in our communities.

WORKING WITH OLDER ADULTS

Working with frail, older adults is a privilege and honor. When our parents or loved ones become older, and in need of more support or attention, it can sometimes be an experience of exhaustion. But, remembering that they were there for us in our infant years, helps us have more understanding about the cycles and circles of life. Life comes full-circle, eventually. It can be a stressful experience when some people are caught in a place when this need of our older loved ones comes at the same time we are raising a family of young ones. Balance becomes very important in this situation. It is those who are living a life that does not have balance, who sometimes do things that cross the line of abuse and neglect… Without intending it. We caregivers must listen to our inner exhaustion and be honest about our human limitations. Maintaining a support group during this time (a few people you can go to or call on a bad day and talk things out) can be helpful.

If someone working with this senior population in an institutional setting does not have this feeling of honor and privilege, they should immediately stop working at this job and find another area of work. Burnout is something that can happen to the best of us. Whether the person is a nurse, administrator, cook, receptionist, maintenance person or

ABUSE AND NEGLECT OF OLDER ADULTS

volunteer – burnout does not know boundaries of role or person. If we can become aware of this exhaustion early on, we may very well be helping to prevent abuse or neglect of older adults that could come from our lack of attention or care, that springs from a place of burnout. Mistakes can happen more frequently among those who stay in a profession after their time for productive work has passed into burnout. Changing roles can be healthy and needed at times of burnout and exhaustion. Change in our lives sometimes requires a soul-searching attitude of reflection. Wisdom in this journey is not found in the soul by adding anything, but rather by taking away distractions and becoming still within ourselves, if possible. Three thousand years ago, the Jewish King David wrote a Psalm (song) that touched on this subject. What he felt was inspired by God came to us today as Psalm 46. "Be still and know that I am God." Reaching out and sharing our feelings with those whom we respect, can be helpful and bring guidance as well.

My time in working with seniors was so refreshing and spiritually, emotionally fulfilling. I stumbled upon a job in a retirement home after working for ten years in the hospice industry. I didn't even know I was burned out from the emotional effects of so many deaths that I had experienced through my work with hospice. Meeting people who were dying, trying to help them and their families did take its toll on my inner life. When you labor with a spiritual earnestness in hospice, saying 'good bye' to people you meet can be difficult. Simply being a loving presence to aid someone in their process of letting go and saying goodbye, can also bring a unique kind of exhaustion and quiet burnout.

Getting a job in a retirement home was so refreshing for me after so many years of working with those who were dying. I loved working with older adults who were not deathly ill, and I

ABUSE AND NEGLECT OF OLDER ADULTS

still cherish memories and stories from that time in my life. In the retirement home where I worked, around 60 people were living in the home. Officially, my job was renting rooms. But unofficially, I was a musician – I kept a guitar in my office, and if someone was feeling low, they knew they could come in and ask me to sing them a song to lift their spirits. Sometimes, they just wanted to sing along. I did this on a regular basis. I sometimes would spontaneously grab my guitar and take a break from my desk work - going into a room where seniors were sitting, just passing the time. There were many lovers of music at this retirement home. I was even able to create a small "choir" from among the residents at Christmas time. We would all dress up with Santa hats and go to the local retirement homes that were "competition" (to the company I worked for). We would sing Christmas carols to seniors – their peers – as they ate lunch or had free time in the afternoon. This was a unique activity and fun to do for everyone. It lifted everyone's spirits and became an excellent service not only to the residents in this particular retirement home but a service to the community. We eventually got requests to sing at church services and funerals during the year. They would bring their "walkers" and sit on them while they sang. Here is a picture of us going out to sing at Christmas. Everyone had a percussion instrument or bells to play while they sang.

ABUSE AND NEGLECT OF OLDER ADULTS

I also helped to create seminars for residents by finding local talent or professionals that were willing to come in for 30 or 40 minutes to share with us on some topic they were an expert in. This helped sharpen and utilize the mental capacities of people who, for the most part, still had a vigorous and healthy mental capacity. Often, their bodies or body parts were not in full active mode, but their minds were sharp and curious. Providing seminars was an excellent service that kept the residents' mental abilities involved and in some cases, kept them informed of new technologies or new movements in society. Sometimes the speaker was the author of a book on the subject, and this helped the older adults feel like they were better informed and up-to-date on the latest trends.

ABUSE AND NEGLECT OF OLDER ADULTS

I was also an avid photographer, and I loved taking pictures of residents that they could share with their families. Cole was so proud of his son and grandson – he talked about them all the time. One day while the three of them were sitting in his room, I asked if I could take a picture of them together. They were delighted. The joy that they felt in being with each other showed on their expressions in the photo. They loved each other so much. Then, the next week, I gave them each a printed copy of the picture. The son confided in me that he felt he was extremely unattractive in photos… But in this picture, he felt that it was "the best photo" he had ever posed for. I assured him it was no trick of lighting or photoshop… It was his countenance of happiness in being with his dad and son. I could capture him at the moment he was genuinely happy, and this was my belief why the photo came out so good. The grandfather showed the picture to everyone, all the time. At his funeral six months later, the picture became a keep sake that I'm sure the son and grandson still cherish.

Then Rita told me that she had no pictures of herself at all. She was single her whole life and felt she was unattractive. But she was wondering if we could do a photo shoot sometime. I knew exactly what I would do with her: outdoors with the beautiful-colored fall trees in the back ground. She had a bright red jacket that fit her well and complimented her thin, snow-white hair. She stood with her walker so proudly. I laid on the ground and shot the photo up, with the colorful maple trees in the background. To this day, I've never seen anyone so appreciative of a photo. She was radiating beauty and proudly displayed the photo on her door. "That's the best picture of me that I've ever had," she said. She had worked her whole life making number two pencils in a factory. That was the only job she ever had – for forty years. No children, no family of her own. As a 'thank you,' she gave me a whole box of pencils that

ABUSE AND NEGLECT OF OLDER ADULTS

she had stored away as a special gift for someone, some day. She had made the pencils herself many years before. They were old. That was the most special gift I had ever received in return for my photography.

Then, one cold and snowy day in February some ladies were looking out the window at all the snow coming down outside, and they started reminiscing about playing in the snow when they were children. "I haven't made a snow man in years," one lady said. "We used to have snowball fights after school," another said. "We used to make snow angels," said another.

After a thoughtful pause, I said to them: ladies, if you want to play in the snow today, I will help you get out there and assist you with your walkers, help you lay down to make snow angels and help you make snow balls for a snow ball fight. And, before you know it (after getting the approval of the head nurse) we were all outside playing in the snow. I can't remember when I had so much fun in the snow. We laughed and carried on for a long time. After a few minutes of fun had passed, I went back inside and grabbed my camera and captured the moment on film. These became the most special memories for everyone. Even the residents who were not well enough to come out with us and play in the snow, all stood by the windows and watched. They cheered us on and laughed with us. It was a topic of conversation for many days.

ABUSE AND NEGLECT OF OLDER ADULTS

ABUSE AND NEGLECT OF OLDER ADULTS

ABUSE AND NEGLECT OF OLDER ADULTS

Then there is the special gift of animals. The unconditional love and genuine affection that a dog or cat can bring into the life of a senior citizen is utterly immeasurable and very helpful (even therapeutic). A total stranger can come into a retirement home or nursing home with his/her pet and soon, everyone is coming to see the animal and say hello. Not all dogs are suited to such an encounter. But, when the animal is appropriate for it, sharing your animal with senior citizens can be one of the easiest things to do. If you are looking for an idea on what you can do to volunteer at your local nursing home, or retirement institution, meet with the leader of the institution. Ask if they would consider the idea of letting you bring a dog or cat to say hello

ABUSE AND NEGLECT OF OLDER ADULTS

to the residents a couple of times per month. My landlady had a dog (below) that I used to bring to work once a week and keep in my office for people to play with and "love on." She was a super gentle dog and very affectionate with everyone.

Every week people knew that if they wanted to give or receive some love from a great dog, they could come to my office on Fridays. Some would volunteer to take her for a walk every two or three hours so she could go to the bathroom. It was so easy to bring her with me to work and so deeply appreciated by so many of the residents and staff. Not all dogs are suited for this sort of service, but if the animal is gentle and mellow, it might be a good thing to try if you have a qualifying pet. In some cities, there are even organizations that will help you "certify" your animal for unique service to the senior citizen, hospice or hospital population. Sadly, this loving dog that is in this

ABUSE AND NEGLECT OF OLDER ADULTS

photograph was deliberately poisoned by people from a secret society after I had written a book that was "not approved" by a secret society called the Illuminati. They killed both my landlady's dog and cat three days apart. According to the police, this animal-murder was a warning not to publish the book I had written. (For more on this story of murder and animal abuse, read my book *"Six Months In Nelson, B.C."*. To read the book they forbid me from publishing, read my book *"Fifty Years of Whispering: LBJ and the alleged killing of JFK."*)

On an entirely different subject, but just as important on a deeper level: I should note to citizens reading this that the general manager at this institution where I worked was a secret society member (Freemason). And, the "head office" was a huge company owned and operated, in large part, by secret society members and their friends/family (secret society symbols were frequently and openly visible in various places at the institution). Furthermore, a percentage of the residents at this retirement home were also secret society members (I can't give you an exact percentage, but it was at least 20 or 30 percent). This institution was expensive and the only families who could afford it were 1) wealthy families (secret society members are usually wealthy) 2) parents that had children who would pay for it or 3) those who saved enough money from working hard their whole life.

One of the residents I got to know was a military man and very open about his connection to the Freemasons. His son and daughter-in-law were also active members of their respective secret societies. While I was working at this residence, (U.S.) Senator Ted Kennedy died. He was a brother of President John Fitzgerald Kennedy and Attorney General Robert Kennedy. When Senator Kennedy died, there was a group of people who went down from Ontario and went to his funeral in

ABUSE AND NEGLECT OF OLDER ADULTS

Massachusetts. At first, I thought that was unusual. But on second thought, I surmised that the Kennedy family was a very famous family and that they had fans from all over the world. When these folks got back from the funeral, it became apparent they were not fans of the Kennedy family at all - but, the complete opposite. They HATED the Kennedy family. This was their report when they got back: "We went down and camped out on the sidewalk, waiting for the funeral procession to pass by with his casket. As the Hearst came by us, we all stood up, and when it got exactly to us, we spit on the ground. I just had to be there and spit on the ground when his dead body came past. Those Kennedy's were assholes, and I hope he's burning in hell." That was the first time I had ever heard someone saying that they went to a funeral of someone they hate. My feeling for that family changed when I listened to that story. They seemed to be saying this as a report to the grandfather who was delighted in hearing this story. He was proud of them. These secret society families carry hate from generation to generation.

I was approached, during my employment at this retirement home, and asked if I'd like to join in with the Freemasons as an official member. I think it important to note that this issue of abuse and neglect of older adults can sometimes be directly tied to secret society members running institutions that are focused more on money and getting rich than they are in the health and happiness of seniors in the community (more on this below). As a human species, people who are members of modern secret societies have failed the human community repeatedly in recent times. We should be very wary of their businesses (which are many), their members (which are many) and their agenda (which is often secretive and clandestine).

If you can, find out who owns and runs the institution you are considering for your loved one, before you get too involved.

ABUSE AND NEGLECT OF OLDER ADULTS

Personally, I never recommend working for people connected to a Freemason or Illuminati network. They bring lots of trouble and heartache to the communities in which they are active. Yes, some of them do "good things." But, they also do evil things (like kill good people who expose their crimes. And, in our day, they are the biggest drug dealers in North America - infecting every community with addiction and social problems connected with drug abuse. They control large parts of the modern day "drug war." For more on this, please read my book *"Six Months In Nelson, B.C."*) I am confident they control the institution where I was working. It was an extensive network of retirement homes all over Canada. The institutional abuse they get away with has affected thousands of elderly citizens.

This 'letter to the editor' is inspired by a very well constructed (and long) paper that was written for the government of Canada by Marie Beaulieu, Ph.D. and Marie-Joseé Tremblay entitled, *"Abuse and Neglect of older adults in institutional settings – A discussion paper building from French language resources."*

Dear Editor,

I recently spent nine months working at a retirement residence in Ontario. On a human level, the experience was great because I had close contact with some great residents. I heard so many stories from their years long past and met some interesting people. On an ethical/institutional level, the experience was sometimes distressing. Private institutions have wide discretionary power over internal regulations. So, organizations can vary widely on levels of abuse and neglect.

ABUSE AND NEGLECT OF OLDER ADULTS

For many seniors, moving to an institution is a difficult choice. In most cases, people have no choice but to leave their homes because of physical challenges (usually they have fallen and broken a bone or suffered a concussion). Others make a move after the death of a spouse because they don't want to live alone.
For many seniors, moving to an institution is a difficult choice.

Since 1992, the Mental Health Division for Health Canada (along with the Federal Family Violence Initiative), has been working collaboratively with many associations, educators and organizations to create resources that deal with the ethics of abuse and neglect in institutional settings. "Ethics" refers to the standards of proper conduct in professional contexts. The purpose of rules is to protect human rights.

Access to information and resources empower older adults and help prevent abuse and neglect. One can reduce social isolation by strengthening resident support systems (like volunteer programs) and providing activities that are exciting and fun. Also, support should be made available to older adults who want to take legal action against an abusive institution or individual. Attorneys who want to help seniors should contact resident councils and offer their services.

THINGS YOU MAY NOT KNOW:

- Most people in a retirement residence are women – approximately 7 to 1. (Therefore, women's groups should be very concerned about what's going on in these institutions).
- The residents in these institutions change over time. When they move in, some have only slight impairments - but these often escalate into severe disabilities.

ABUSE AND NEGLECT OF OLDER ADULTS

- The average length of stay in a retirement residence is four years (costing at least $30,000 annually). Four years will cost around $120,000. What this means for most people, is that moving to a retirement residence becomes the second biggest purchase most people make in their entire life. It's a significant life moment.
- Many residents report an increase in their quality of life when innovative programs (such as music therapy and animal therapy) are regularly used. Having volunteers who bring animals and musical instruments are a huge asset in helping seniors feel a higher quality life.

PREVENTION

Abuse and neglect of older adults is a social problem that concerns everyone. Unfortunately, it is all too often covered up in a cloak of silence. Public awareness of abuse encourages reporting and makes people more aware of the possibility of inadequate treatment. Detecting ill-treatment and neglect of older adults must be the responsibility of everyone in the community.

Providing education and training on the aging process, referring a family to respite services (everybody needs a break from the stress and challenges of caregiving), and supplying technical and moral support services can do much to prevent abuse. Compared with thirty years ago, much more is known today about ill-treatment and neglect of older adults. So, we are headed in the right direction. However, much remains to be done. Raising awareness is one of the keys to fighting abuse in institutional settings. Hence, public conversation is key (for example, letters to the editor). Burnout among staff can also spiral into mistreatment – so it becomes necessary to be aware

ABUSE AND NEGLECT OF OLDER ADULTS

of burnout and emotional overload. Another prevention strategy consists of breaking social isolation. It is here that volunteers play an important and vital role.

VOLUNTEERS

Creating support systems and bonds among volunteers and residents can increase confidence in residents and (coincidently) raises the level of reporting.

Peer relations are critical in detecting abuse and neglect, as older adults sometimes find it easier to be open with each other. For many older adults, it is simpler to talk to peers than to staff members, who are, more often than not, seen as authority figures. Volunteers are often seen and experienced as caring and fun friends. Social change can only be achieved by collectively sharing responsibility.

AUTONOMY

Preventative measures are only useful to the extent that residents have real decision-making powers in these resident committees. Resident committees in institutions give older adults a role and an opportunity to assert their rights. We must recognize their contributions and allow them to maintain their autonomy as much as possible. The higher the level of feeling 'autonomous' is directly proportional to a higher level of 'quality of life'.

By putting into place, a resident committee (with real decision-making powers), institutions provide an opportunity for honest discussions about issues that matter to the residents. Doing this

ABUSE AND NEGLECT OF OLDER ADULTS

can help create a feeling of autonomy and positive self-worth or positive self-regard.

Freedom and autonomy within an institution can be tricky. How much freedom can you give within an institution? For example, why aren't residents or resident committees consulted about the arrangement of furnishings or paintings in their rooms (both public and private rooms)? Why can't they choose when they have a bath? Is it a healthy thing to not tell them when there has been a death of a loved one? The list of questions regarding autonomy can be lengthy.

One thing is for certain: Administrators and staff can quickly forget that they are only visitors in these communities. Since they are only visitors, humility and deference can be very appropriate attitudes used to carry out one's daily duties. Whether volunteer or paid staff, everyone is here to serve.

In searching government documents online, I was looking for a definition of "institutional abuse" regarding seniors. I wanted to do something about the systemic neglect I was witnessing at the institution where I worked. But, I was unable to find any commonly accepted definition of what constitutes ill-treatment of seniors – the terms that frequently appear: 'abuse,' 'neglect,' 'violence' and 'mistreatment.'

The bad treatment is not limited to physical harm, however, but also includes psychological abuse (which includes all behavior that undermines the older adult's identity, dignity or self-confidence). Abuse can also be financial shadiness or material exploitation and neglect of health and personal needs (which includes the intentional administration of medication which could impair the health of older adults by making them listless or apathetic). It's important that Administrators and managers know what their role is when it comes to developing strategies and training programs to help prevent abuse and neglect. Sadly, it seems to be a low priority for some leaders of institutions.

TRAINING

The truth is, abusers are often unfamiliar with the needs of older adults, or they lack experience/training when dealing with the needs of people in this demographic. No doubt about it - what we need in institutions is more proper training. For many staff members, such training is not only skill enhancing but an absolute necessity. Through training, their knowledge of the aging process can improve the quality of a residents' life. "Abusers" are not always "bad" people. Often, they are good people with bad training (or no training at all). Often, they are just working with the only tools they have. If the only tool you have is a hammer, every problem becomes a nail. Once employees get proper training, they may learn that there are other alternatives besides yelling at a resident (for example).

Training sessions are one of the best ways to raise awareness on a wide variety of issues. Institutions must make education of staff and volunteers a continual and constant priority. To a large extent, organizations take the lead from their head office leadership. It is important for the institution to send a message to all caregivers, mandating them not to ignore signs of abuse. But, what happens if the abuse is systematic – originating from policies or pressure from head office?

I'll give you an example: The recent employee cutbacks at the institution where I worked were massive. Of course, cuts are going to happen during times like these (2009). However, "head office" anticipated that residents would be distraught when their rent went up 5% and hundreds of staff hours would

ABUSE AND NEGLECT OF OLDER ADULTS

be cut for the second time in a year. At a conference for managers in the network, managers were told: "raising the rent will allow us to recover money lost due to the inflation of prices (food prices go up, water prices go up, etc.) and the cut in staff hours will allow the investors to make good money on their investment." It's true that companies have a moral obligation to their investors. But when it comes to seniors and children, the standards companies use must be different. In most businesses, the investors are more important than the clients. This is not true when it comes to companies that serve children and seniors.

When this "return on investment" conflicts with the needs of seniors... and crosses the line of abuse and neglect, we must stand up and remind companies their top priority in a business, like retirement residences, is to serve seniors first - not investors. What is needed is more creative thinking - not shady practices that encourage neglect and abuse. "Head office" then instructed (and pressured) all 200+ managers in their network to spend more time working from their home. The reasoning behind this, they explained, was that they didn't want any managers spending their time hearing complaints about all the cutbacks. This new rule is a good example of bad leadership and bad service to seniors. The government of Canada is allowing this go on.

From October to February I rarely saw the general manager (Mr. M.A.). Residents would come to me asking if they could talk to him. I'd go looking for him, and he'd left the building (like he was Elvis!). He was hiding at his home from residents and staff! Residents would want to talk to him and ask why their rent went up 5% and he was gone. Residents wanted to complain about this or that, and he was not around. It was evident that General Managers were told to work from their homes as well. I complained to head office that managers

ABUSE AND NEGLECT OF OLDER ADULTS

abandoning a property of seniors was a form of neglect and thus, illegal. They eventually fired me for being "too negative." Some employees left or were encouraged to leave. It was a sad and emotional time for many of the residents who were trying to deal with so many significant changes in such a short span of time. (I learned that it's true: The older you get, the harder "change" becomes).

Luckily, for the residents, not all the excellent people left – but all the remaining staff were united on one thing: they were deeply concerned about how "head office was treating residents". Residents told me about one of their favorite nurses getting fired for speaking out about the unethical mandates. I knew of another highly qualified nurse who recently quit because she felt that head office was asking her to do things that were unethical. If these companies keep losing good employees from among their best and most dedicated, that's not good business practice. If all the good employees left behind are in a spiral of low morale, what will that do to the quality of life of seniors in these institutions? How can these companies attract good people and retain them? Does head office even realize they are losing some of their most dedicated people on the front lines?

Residents are not stupid. They are aware that staff is becoming smaller and that they have less time to devote to residents. Older adults all too often feel like a burden to family and friends already. These cutbacks make many of them feel like an even bigger burden on the overworked staff who are now drowning in low morale and lack of respect for the head office.

Seniors are often considered a burden because they do not participate actively in economic production. The lack of connection between generations may be one reason why older adults are 1) more isolated and 2) often perceived as a burden.

ABUSE AND NEGLECT OF OLDER ADULTS

Some people don't understand their significant psychosocial contribution to the community. While life expectancy has increased considerably – medical progress has extended the life span, but the final years are not always healthy and pain-free. Some seniors live in constant pain (both physical and emotional). Science has added years to our life – but it's up to us to help seniors find life and meaning during those years. Isolation and loneliness are epidemics in these institutions. We should all care about this. Social change can only be achieved by collectively sharing responsibility.

Monitoring is an effective means for preventing and correcting abuse, and many of these private institutions are unmonitored. Head office can pressure managers to abandon the property - work from home - and no one says anything about this blatant abandoning of massive numbers of seniors. Even though the GM was available by phone, this is not an efficient or helpful way to deal with the day to day concerns that come up for seniors. Would society accept a parent who never comes home and monitors their children by the phone? Of course not!

If we are going to serve seniors, we must first help them gain control over the organization of their lives. We can't do this by working with them from our homes, over the phone. When we do genuinely help them gain control over their lives, we work with them from our hearts, not for them over the phone.

Dillon Woods

ABUSE AND NEGLECT OF OLDER ADULTS

The following are emails I received in response to the above "letter to the editor":

Hi Dillon,

I have checked out your letter to the editor. I was sorry to hear that you are no longer there, my mother really liked you. Things have really changed around there since you left!! My mom was never one to sit back if she doesn't like something and speaks up for herself. She has become the spokesperson for those who complain but won't do anything about it.

Since my experience with placing my mom at the residence, many acquaintances have come to me for advice, it's something my age group is now facing, and the realization of the hurdles to overcome is mind boggling. Until I was confronted and dealt with the issues of a "retirement home" I had no idea of the complications surrounding them and the behind-the-scenes goings-on. The waiting lists are endless (3 years!) for a suitable subsidized facility, and we have talked about finding another place but as you know seniors are reluctant and do not adapt to change quickly. To face the possibility of her living with me in the future would be a hardship as I wasn't able to care for her 2yrs ago when she could no longer manage her own home.

I found it ironic that one of the premiers (or some government official) was in the same shoes a few years ago with an aging parent but of course given who he was, does not have to face the challenges and difficulties the average Canadian does...

Keep up the good work.

ABUSE AND NEGLECT OF OLDER ADULTS

Hi Dillon,

I read your article, which I'm sure refers to your time at the residence where my parents live. It's been such a loss to lose you from the staff there. You certainly brought 'joie de vivre' and much light to the entire place, and you are very much missed.

Everything you've said in your article really does 'hit the nail on the head', so sometimes using a hammer is a good thing. It's distressing for both the residents and their families. It seems to me that the residents always feel like they are being 'herded' around with no real thought for their quality of life. Abrupt staff and program changes really affect them emotionally and leave them floundering. It's distressing for family members as we rely on the quality of the care and programming so that our parent (s) can thrive. When we question what is happening, we are given little if no information and a resident's "complaint form" to write a brief comment on, is a tiny post card with a couple of lines. In other words, the administration is giving us "the run around."

The focal point of your article hinges on the fact that 'head office' is making decisions based on their "shareholders" pocketbooks versus what their clients need, so that despite the substantial increase in fees, the level of service and care is purposively decreased, creating even more of a stress on present employees. The problem becomes circular with the residents, who make the business possible with their fees, having a lower level of service, less quality of life and being generally distressed.

ABUSE AND NEGLECT OF OLDER ADULTS

Obviously, with many aging seniors in our population base, "Seniors" have become "BIG Business." What suggestions do you have? If one had the intention to improve the quality of life for seniors living in residential facilities what would be some of the things to do to ensure that this is a priority that starts with senior management of the parent companies and is then fostered in the local residences?

Best regards,

DILLON'S RESPONSE:

Good questions. I've been thinking ... and the only good answer I can come up with is to force these companies to have 5% of their staff hours be volunteer hours. We must force these companies (or reward them) to create good volunteer programs. Volunteers will help solve many issues on many levels.

Second, I think lawsuits need to be launched against these big companies who are neglecting seniors. But, lawsuits take money. In this society, only a lawsuit will get the attention of the "suits" at head office. Once this happens, they will change their tune.

Also, I think protesting at investor meetings would be appropriate. Do investors know that these companies are equal to companies who abuse children to create products? Profiting from the abuse/neglect of seniors is just like profiting from the abuse of children who work in sweat shops. Exposing the actions of "suits" to their investors should make these "suits" hang their heads in shame and encourage them to change their behavior.

ABUSE AND NEGLECT OF OLDER ADULTS

Hi, Dillon!

The "letter to the editor" is excellent. You've exactly outlined the situation at this residence correctly. I am currently in the process of writing a letter to the head office with copies to ORCA and my member of parliament (which I will copy to you now as well).

My mother was recently hospitalized with complications from cancer but is back living at the residence now. She currently is having her meals in her room as she isn't strong enough to get dressed or go downstairs. The other day I called from work at 2:45 in the afternoon to ask her how she was feeling and she told me she was still waiting for lunch! Earlier in the morning, I was there meeting the CCAC but at 9:50 when her breakfast hadn't come up I excused myself and went downstairs to get it myself. Dinner had been brought up at 6:45 pm the day before and was stone cold. Very often her bed doesn't get made, and she has to call down for clean towels.

I went ballistic! Of course, the GM isn't on the property to talk to. This GM was hired after the other one left, but didn't start for a month because she had 'pneumonia' and now she's on a two-week vacation in Paris?! When I spoke with the DOC she lied and told me that they have the same amount of staff as before but when I continued pressuring her she finally admitted the truth: that there had been some big cutbacks in staff hours. I said that RA's should not be running into the kitchen and dining room to serve, nor should the maintenance man be in the kitchen in his dirty work clothes serving food to the residents. This must be a health violation! I told the DOC I was tired of this, not just for Mom's sake but all the residents there. The rent

ABUSE AND NEGLECT OF OLDER ADULTS

went up yet again but the services and quality of life at the residence has declined and continues to.

Up until this point, I didn't want to complain too much in case my parent's care would be jeopardized. Dillon, keep up the fight. I decided 30 years ago that the atrocities I saw my aunt and grandmother go thru in nursing homes would never happen to my parents. I realized then that something had to be done to change things. We've come a long way since then but there are still more changes to be made and the only way that can happen is if we, as a community, are involved. Thanks for your efforts to alert and encourage the public to get involved.

Take care,

Dillon Woods is an author, journalist, musician, and filmmaker. He is the author of many books. For more information on his work, go to http://www.SecretSocietiesSuck.com, https://www.amazon.com, or https://www.youtube.com.

Printed in Dunstable, United Kingdom